A Small Book of Universal Wisdom

A Small Book
of
Universal Wisdom

ANNIE JAMESON

A SMALL BOOK OF UNIVERSAL WISDOM

First published by Higher Realms Publishing (NZ), Hamilton, New Zealand, in 2008
P O Box 21047, Hamilton, 3249, New Zealand
email: annie@higher-realms.co.nz www.higher-realms.co.nz

ISBN 978-0-473-14360-2

Printed in New Zealand

Design by Ruby Red Design, Tauranga
Author's Photograph by Jane Sheldon, Hamilton
Printed by Kale Print and Design, Tauranga

Cover Image: Alpha Centauri
"Digital Sky Survey/David Malin Images"
More details of this image on http://www.aao.gov.au/images/captions/dss004.html

Contents

7	CHAPTER ONE	Awakening of the soul
15	CHAPTER TWO	Symbols for your mind
23	CHAPTER THREE	Raising consciousness
29	CHAPTER FOUR	Thought forms
39	CHAPTER FIVE	Life's journey
47	CHAPTER SIX	You are not alone
52	CHAPTER SEVEN	Opening your heart
57	CHAPTER EIGHT	Healing
71	CHAPTER NINE	Shining your light

Dedication

To my beautiful mother Astri, with deep love and gratitude

Gratitude

It is with deep appreciation and gratitude that I honour the ascended masters who are the true authors of this book.

I am so grateful to my beloved husband Michael for being my anchor and surrounding me with so much love and encouragement in bringing this book to fruition.

And so many hugs to our wonderful sons Ben and Sam, who are a constant source of love, wisdom and humour.

Special thanks to Robyn McCarroll (of Ruby Red Design) for once again producing such beautiful artwork.

So many thanks also go to my family and friends who continuously encourage me in so many ways to follow my spiritual path. I thank each of you.

Finally as always I am truly blessed and thankful to Chilao and the angelic realms that inspire and guide me in every way.

Blessings and love to you all.

Introduction

When we take the time to immerse ourselves in the silence of meditation we begin to receive the guidance we seek and tap into Divine wisdom. This is how my journey began in 1991 when I made the decision to focus more on my inward spiritual journey. In prayer and meditation I asked to be connected with my Guardian Angel and this turned out to be the most profound decision I have ever made in my life. I discovered that I could conduct a dialogue through a clear channel of communication with my Guardian Angel Chilao and the higher spiritual realms. I came to trust that I was receiving Divine guidance on a daily basis as the information rang so true within me. Some of this writing has been published in my first book "The Light of Chilao - Messages from Heaven".

This connection has deepened over the years as I continued to meditate. When I asked how I could better serve humanity as a whole I began to receive a series of channelled teachings from the ascended masters. In this book they discuss ways to move through the blocks that we unconsciously create in our lives, helping us to see them as gifts and opportunities for growth. This has proved to be invaluable in seeing the bigger picture in every situation I face and in making wiser decisions in my life.

I believe each of us has the ability to receive Divine guidance, and as we are all different, so each person will experience this in different ways. As each of us consciously chooses to embrace the light within then we can move forward to creating a better future that encompasses so much more than we settled for before.

So it is that I invite you to use this Small Book of Universal Wisdom to help you gain a deeper understanding of your life.   As you contemplate a particular situation then the teachings in this book can inspire you to make decisions from a more centred space. This book does not need to be read from beginning to end; another option is to ask to be guided then open the book intuitively and contemplate on the words you read. If you allow yourself to be guided by your heart and let the intellectual mind soften, you may find that life will flow more easily for you.

Annie

CHAPTER ONE

Awakening of the soul

NOW IS the time that a full awakening is needed upon Earth. As each person recognizes the spark of God within, then they can expand this consciousness more fully to encompass the light.

Imagine looking down upon a city in the darkness of the night. Gradually lights will flicker on in people's homes as they awaken to the morning light. One after the other lights will come on and brighten up their homes from the darkness. See this as a symbol to understand fully the awakening of the soul. As the light comes on from within you it will begin to shine fully upon your day ahead. There will be clarity as you move about with more focus than ever before. The fumbling in the darkness shall be no more for the light will shine so brightly. This will in turn uncover all that needs to be healed from within.

This is the only way forward to move you out of the reverie and dream-like state you have fallen into. Each of you needs to reach for this light switch within you and consciously make an effort to turn it on. No longer can you drift in a dream state, not taking the responsibility for your actions, words and deeds.

When the light shines brightly you can no longer fumble along in a stupor. This is the awakening from within. As you bring this more fully into your consciousness you will see the plan ahead. It is no longer "each for your own" that will not suffice. Brush away the sleep from your eyes and take responsibility for what you now see before you. See your life as never before, by seeing it with clarity. Let go of the drama, the re-creation of the same patterns and lower thought forms. They shall and will drag you down into the mud, so to speak.

With mud in your eyes how can you truly see the plan for humanity?

Open the channel between

Heaven and Earth;

you no longer need to

feel the separation

How can you be of service in any way? To yourself be true, honour this path of awakening. Even as you have the intent to gingerly step onto your path of light, it is the intention that will blast the way forward for you.

The responsibility for all you have created in your life, whether you perceive it to be good or bad, is what will shift your focus. Today begin as you have never begun before, by setting your intent higher to reach your highest goals. Do not settle for less, it will not suffice anymore. You will feel and know that your heart is opening, maybe a crack at a time. Soon your heart will be fully awakened; you will not want to settle for less.

As the consciousness of each person rises in conjunction with the raising of awareness of the whole of humanity, new sights may be set. Your planet Earth is but a speck on the horizon of the vastness of the Universe, see it expanding in your mind. Now, do not see it with darkness or despair but rather saturate it with your love. Know that your one and only thought form will make a difference; see it in your mind as the lighting of a candle. As each candle holds the light, the flame shall shine and bring more light. These candles are symbols for your hearts; open your hearts and let the love pour through you. Open the channel between Heaven and Earth;

you no longer need to feel the separation. This is not in truth, for in reality there is no separation. In the Universe we are all one, each planet revolves in accordance with the Divine Energy.

As you begin to see the vastness of the Universe as but a speck in your mind's eye, fill and saturate it with your love. This will radiate outwards to encompass all forms of life. It is in the act of holding the Earth and the Universe in this higher state of consciousness that the healing will begin.

Compassion for mankind is needed from the deepest level of your soul. Do not be caught in the drama and darkness. Lower thought forms will drag you down to that level. Only hold the light in your mind's eye and see the planet as whole. See the sun, moon and all the planets vibrating in accordance with All That Is; this is the way forward. Seeing the Earth as whole again will enable the healing to happen. As each of you holds your soul in reverence, as the soul you truly are, then you will rise to the challenge. For indeed it is only a challenge. Do you step forward with intent to meet it or do you step back? It is your choice, your free will to do as you feel the strongest energy.

Let not another day go by without making the conscious choice to act with integrity and truth in all you do. State this firmly and the energy that will mirror this will come into your lives. Feel the energy around

*See your growth as
a seedling, as a plant
you are nurturing*

you, wake up to the feeling within. You no longer need to be numb with pain or fear this no longer serves you. Your soul is awakening; it has the strength to move you out of this reverie, this comfort zone. It only takes one positive choice to no longer accept this in your life.

Look at how you may serve others when you are in pain or fear. This will shift you out of the lower vibration and flood your being with light. Every act, deed or thought that is of a higher vibration will in turn nourish your own soul. See your growth as a seedling, as a plant you are nurturing. As it begins to grow you do not leave it to become arid and dry, no, you water and tend to it. So too tend to the growth of your soul. Each newly formed shining leaf unfurling is another step on your way. The healing shall come to you as you lovingly look after yourself. From this unlimited energy and overflowing love can you then give to another. When you feel unloved and dry inside how can there be an overflow, for there is not enough to nourish you.

So begin today honouring yourself, pay attention to the thoughts and ideas that start to form in your mind. Your mind gives you mixed messages when it is cluttered and overactive. How can you make clear decisions when your mind is brimming over with clutter and rubbish? As in a room that is full of clutter, how can you focus, the energy is one of distraction. Know how different you feel when you tidy up and have a good spring clean. See then also that your mind needs a daily spring clean too. Do not let the dust settle until it is so fixed it cannot move easily. Cleanse your mind daily, imagine a broom sweeping all the rubbish away and start afresh. Choose carefully what you will fill it with. You would be much more careful once your room is cleaned, you would not consider then emptying your rubbish into the middle of it. Then so too do not do this to your mind, for it is very susceptible to what you put there. Your mind is like a sponge and will soak up whatever input it is given. This is truly important for each of you to clear this clutter, mire and distortion out of your minds and lives.

Do not let your mind take control any longer, command that it be still. Nourish it with uplifting words and visions. Fill it daily with positive energy and burn away and dump the rest. See the gold, silver and violet flame transmute all the rubbish. As this becomes a conscious act in your life you will free yourself of the bonds you have tied yourself up with.

No one is responsible for you, there is no one that is in control of you or your thoughts, but you. State this firmly to yourself that you are willing to fill your mind and your life with positive vibrations. This is the way forward to help yourself and in turn help humanity.

CHAPTER TWO

Symbols for your mind

SEE YOURSELVES as a tiny speck in the Universe, a spark from God. Now as you begin to visualize this spark of light expanding and radiating outwards, see the light spread before you. As a shooting star spreads its light as it dances across the sky, see yourself in this way also, in a position of spreading your light far and wide.

Out of the darkness shall your light shine, transmuting all fear and

Bless each situation in

your own lives as a gift

and you will see the perfect

solution in everything

lower vibrations. For within the light darkness cannot reside, this is the key for humanity. As each person raises their consciousness, bringing this light with them to shine brighter and brighter, then they shall radiate light to touch all hearts that lie ahead.

Using these powerful symbols for your minds will create this light fully and raise the consciousness of Man. From this perspective the light within even the darkest mind shall illuminate the soul. As each of you raises your own vibration, this shall indeed trigger a response from the next person you encounter. It shall be their free choice to respond or not, however you have given them the opportunity, the chance to see life differently.

In all countries around the world there are those holding to this force of light, and as each of you wherever you are bring this energy to the fore it shall increase and expand outwards. You will be sending forth a grid of light that will encapsulate all of humanity, with bridges and paths of light upon which angels may walk in abundance. As the angelic realm is invoked to surround your Earth, so the consciousness of humanity may be raised. Each individual has their own power to link to the God force within and bring this energy up and outwards to link to the Divine.

Bless each situation in your own lives as a gift and you will see the perfect solution in everything. Everybody with whom you meet, see each connection as a gift, an opportunity to pass something positive on to them. Imagine how this shall be with every handshake, with every hug, and with every word of communication, that the light of healing is carried from one to another.

This indeed is truly a gift to humanity. As every thought, word and deed carries a powerful energy, then so charge it with the light. Imagine a small child receiving this gift of light in their tiny hands. This they will feel, for they are more in tune with the God force within them and shall feel the vibration like a shining star of light.

Fill your minds and hearts with these simple visualizations. As you sit next to someone on a bus, a park bench or standing in a queue, begin to practice this powerful visualization. As the speech flows forth from your mouth, visualize stars of light flowing out to touch another. Feel the vibration of the words you utter, do they uplift you or drag you down? Be conscious in all you do, this is a gift to truly understanding each of your fellow men. Does not each soul deserve to be uplifted when they are down? For the inner consciousness that resides deep within each of you can and shall be awakened. Each of you deserves to bring this love and compassion to yourselves and in turn to others.

*The path of light back
to God is where your soul
will ultimately lead you*

Speak always your truth; use the Divine Energy that radiates within you to lift another; it takes but a matter of a second to share this gift.

Feel the God presence rising up within each of you as you take back your power. Stand firm in your beliefs, those of truth and let all else fall away. To bring yourselves into alignment with these higher energies will align each and every one of you with your true path. As the soul's journey unfolds it bends and sways with the tides. As the tide flows in and out, so too the soul flows with each situation that has been created for its ultimate growth. The path of light back to God is where your soul will ultimately lead you.

Stand always in your truth and integrity, and know that this is the only way forward on this path of light. For as you feel deep within yourselves this inner longing to be more aligned to the God-force, then it shall be so.

The awakening is happening now for humanity. More than at any other time the soul is challenged to make this step, either to follow the light or to fall away. For nothing but the true love of God can stand in the light. The light of God shall blaze forth and literally saturate your soul. It shall be cleansed and brought into alignment. This must come from your own choosing. This is a time of Oneness with God, All That

Speak always your truth;

use the Divine Energy

that radiates within you

to lift another

Is; all else shall fade away. You shall each be illuminated from within and without for all to truly see. As on the inner planes all is revealed, so too now as humanity wakes up out of its deep reverie all shall be revealed.

Each of you shall be able to stand before one another and truly see the spark of God rising and shining within. The light shall transmute all darkness and shadows will fade away in this light. People shall be able to see deep within the soul. There will be a true recognition of who you really are, not on the surface but deep within the soul.

Stand up now to be counted and follow your true path of enlightenment to be one with God, All That Is.

CHAPTER THREE

Raising your consciousness

TRUST IN the implicitness of God's love for that is where you will all gain your source of strength.

Now is the time for all of humanity to move through the bonds of fear. Your planet Earth is surrounded in waves of energy that vibrate in accordance with All That Is.

In areas of your planet Earth there are parts that have a stronger more

Trust in the implicitness

of God's love for that is

where you will all gain

your source of strength

positive vibration and all standing in realms of awareness shall see this. On the inner planes it is plain for all to see. There is a flow and harmony with all that is. In general the thought forms have been raised to a higher consciousness of awareness.

In other areas it is dry and lacking, withering and floundering with uncertainties and fear. Those who vibrate in these lower realms are manifesting all that they are putting out. For the Universal Law states that what you put out you will receive.

All it takes is one consciousness to snowball and reach others to give them hope. It is in the awakening of people to see that they are truly creating the mire and distortion in parts of the planet. As all is whole and resonates as one, each affects another.

See now how vitally important it is that a mass awakening occur to raise the vibration of the planet, to disperse the mass negativity that is creating their miserable existence. For all of you are responsible for what is showing up in your lives. There are indeed no victims; this is all in your own doing. It is the lack of awareness that it can be another way.

How should it be if a spark of golden light touched one in this place of sadness? This would magnify and spread joy with all who came into contact with that one person. See today how each of you can be responsible and have the consciousness to choose the path of light. As Jesus Christ walked upon the Earth and shone his light of All That Is so too can each of you be a living master of the light.

No matter how small or how great the deed of love to another, know that you may have ignited the spark of God and the Christ consciousness within them. Fill your hearts with true deep love for all of humanity and let peace reside among you in light, love, thought, word and deed.

It is now time to bring in the higher energies to saturate the Earth. The more people that raise their consciousness the greater the shift can be for the Earth. It is extremely important, vital, for the masses to awaken and know who they truly they are and why they have chosen to incarnate at this time. For as each person reaches out and grasps their purpose fully, so once again the wheel of life can turn a full circle. This is a great opportunity for each individual in his or her own growth. Some will sit back and ignore this opening and others of you will grasp this fully and move towards the light.

It is in the act of service to each other that you shall grow more fully. The time has come to dissolve away pettiness or small mindedness and see the greater picture. It is not each for your own anymore this will not suffice. One cannot go round in a fog anymore. The way is clearing for

It is in the act of service

to each other that you

shall grow more fully

those who can see and choose to see clearly. It is with clarity the path ahead is seen and shown to you.

There is no time for fear and hesitation. This is a chance in this lifetime that planetary alignments are such as to bring these openings. Trust that as you ask for guidance everyday that you be surrounded with protection and light that it shall be. This way you shall each move forward with courage. It is the way of the Ancient Ones. Be in your power, step out and make a difference in this lifetime.

CHAPTER FOUR

Thought forms

VISUALIZE THE Earth spread before you and then see in your mind it begin to shrink, as though you are now able to place it gently in the palm of your hand. As this energy has come into a manageable size you are able to saturate it with your love. Surrounding and protecting the sphere of the Earth with this radiant energy everyday will allow a release of all the toxic thought forms held in it's structure.

The world, as you know it, has over the centuries been filled with toxic thought forms by the masses. This in turn becomes ingrained into the earth's structure and energy fields around the planet. This needs to be transmuted fully for the planet Earth to be freed.

Each and every one of you can play your part. It is vital that the loving energy be sent out to dissolve this negative matter that has attached to the Earth. As each of you focuses your pure intent to heal the Earth, so a grid of light is formed and strengthened. Gradually these thought forms are dissolved in the light, Universal Law will prevail.

It is vital that each of you see this as part of the Divine plan to raise the consciousness of humanity. You each have your part to play. Those who are not ready will indeed have their wake up call. It shall be their choice, their freewill whether to follow the light or stay plunged in darkness. These may feel like rocky times, but in truth these times are momentous for humanity.

A vital shift in consciousness shall raise you into the fifth dimension as a whole. Take care of your brothers and sisters. Give them the opportunity to raise their consciousness. For it is in the opening of the doorway that they will finally see with eyes of truth and understanding. They will not wonder anymore, but rather look at their own lives and the healing shall begin. It only takes but a peep to capture their imagination to see what their lives could be truly like. When they stand in their power they will see their lives unfold as petals of a flower awakening to a new dawn.

Refresh these parts of yourself by daily affirming your intent to carry the light. Affirm that your intention be to carry a higher consciousness to raise people's awareness throughout the day. It only takes but a few words of kindness to uplift someone from their darkest moment. For indeed the darkness that is carried by some resides in their thought forms. Blast through this with a positive statement that is loving and kind, and you will see that you have made a difference.

Let all of humanity work together as a whole. Each of you has your own journey, your own paths of growth. However as a whole you can lift your planet Earth to the higher dimensions. All fear and pain held in its core can be transmuted and in turn lift humanity.

Every living thing vibrates to the tune of its own drum, as each of you picks up the pace of the drum, you will see your lives speed up in the most positive way. Release the package of energy that is holding you down, dragging your feet as though a lead weight is upon you. Break those chains of despair and choose to walk freely giving out to all those you meet.

It only takes but a few words of kindness to uplift someone from their darkest moment

You are all responsible for the uplifting of Earth and humanity. Each of you does not function without the other. Do not lean on your brothers and sisters to pull you along and rescue you continuously. That is but a pattern of despair. It is only when each of you accepts responsibility for your own mind and what it is creating that you shall move into the light.

Visualize each thought form as a balloon going out into the atmosphere. Is yours going out carrying a strong energy of love, light and harmony or is it going out and polluting the atmosphere with fear, anger or other lower thought forms? Use your imagination to perceive what this would look like from where you stand upon Earth. For indeed this is how it is seen on the inner planes. Either as a puff of pollution clogging up and attracting to it even lower vibrations or as light attracting to it all that is good. What you think shall go out as a boomerang and come back to you immediately. You will not expect it and least of all realize it is in your own creation.

Every choice you make has an impact on the rest of humanity. Do not wallow anymore as the victim or sufferer. Stand up and take yourself seriously as one who holds integrity, truth and the light. Go forth into this world of yours with this energy and see the wonder that will spread before you.

Each person can play his or her part in uplifting humanity. As you focus within to release all blockages that are holding you back then this energy will ricochet outwards to the Divine. As this energy is transmuted instantaneously, then so too that vibration will go outwards and imprint an energy into the ethers. As you visualize this release within yourself, know too that on a very deep level this is having an impact on humanity and the universe.

All is interlinked; this multidimensional energy is linked to the whole, to the Source. As an orange has segments that fit together as a whole, so are each of you part of a whole. As you state forth the intention of bringing yourself into alignment with the Source, then so too can the energy of each of you come into alignment once again to form part of the whole.

See a seed before you and as you know that the Divine plan of energy is already contained within that seed, then know too that this symbolizes yourself. Within each of you is the genetic coding and structure that will form in the perfect Oneness with God and All That Is. From this perception and understanding then know that within you is the structure that will form in alignment with God with the highest will you can achieve.

For within your free will you each have a choice to be in alignment or to choose otherwise.

You cannot from this space, time or energy then judge another for you will truly see only that which is of the Divine within each person. From this viewpoint all is perfect and in order with the Universal theme and the highest vibration will be understood. Hold this thought, this energy vibration and link to the Divine at all times and you will see the magnificence of God working perfectly in every way.

Judgment is of a lower vibration, a lower thought form; it is but a trap. See past this and make a conscious choice not to fall for it, strike it aside and revoke all that is not pure. This is the only way to overcome this essence that can drag each of you down. It is but a snare that gets people caught in a web of despair, of not understanding why they are here on Earth. Break free of these strands of energy they no longer serve you. They will not sit in the same energy field or vibration with you as you cast them aside to the Christ within. You all know, every one of you, what feels in truth and what does not. Make this a continual balancing process, make it part of your daily routine. As you keep your bodies clean so too cleanse your mind of all lower thought forms, remove the traps one by one. As you perceive them and see them for what they are release them to be transmuted into the Light of the Christ consciousness. All will be transmuted instantaneously and removed from your energy field.

As the energy rises and falls within each of you so this energy shall be attuned to the Earth. For the amount of energy you put forth in a positive way will have a beneficial impact on the Earth. So too shall it be that negative or lower vibrational energy will have a negative impact on the structure of the Earth.

As each person becomes aware that their words are indeed actions in spirit form, so they may curb their tongues more often and so also their thoughts. Each thought form is a living vibration that goes out and hangs in the air around you. Therefore this shall show you how important, how vital it is to censor your thoughts before they become destructive. As each person can lift his or her own energy in this way, then each becomes responsible for themself. Then they will know from a deep level of understanding about thought forms and how they manifest to produce either good or negative results.

There is nothing happening by chance on your planet Earth and there are many strings and cords to be broken to avoid the same mistakes made by humanity as a whole. It is indeed by the power of man's words and

Judgment is of a

lower vibration,

a lower thought form;

it is but a trap

thoughts that actions have manifested with either good or bad intent. Once this understanding has been felt on a deeper level then so too can Man take control of his planet Earth again.

The planet Earth is unsupported; it is under attack from every angle mostly from people's subconscious selves. There is no knowing or understanding of what it means to be of service for many. This needs to be awakened in people for the spiral of the wheel to turn and move forward. Bringing this awareness to people's consciousness is vital if you are to divert catastrophes in the future. Let every man not be an island all alone, but rather move, bend and sway with the flow of life. @

CHAPTER FIVE

Life's journey

AS YOU see your life spread before you, you will see the signposts also ahead of you. With clear eyes you will recognize the signs and know truly which way to turn. It is only in the fog that comes from your mind that these signposts become hazy and in some cases totally obliterated. It is at these times when you fumble and feel your way desperately seeking for help.

As you so believe it,

so all in your life shall

manifest accordingly

As you tune into the greater dimensions of light that pours down from the Heavens, God's shining light, you then cannot fail to see each step ahead so clearly. Lift up your sights higher, above the fog and mire of your minds for these are but a distraction. The veils will separate you as you insist upon being stuck behind the curtain that blankets out the glory that is set before you.

Each of you has the ability to truly see with clear eyes. It is in these choices that you may move forward. As you can see on a foggy day you move slowly about testing out gently which way to go. Then at these times state forth your positive intention that God and the Angels lift these veils away from you so that once again you may truly see.

You do not need to act out the role of underdog for all to tread upon. Lift your vibration with intention. You are not the victim; this is a figment of your imagination. For as you so believe it, so all in your life shall manifest accordingly. It is the statement of bringing the power deep within into alignment with God that you shall move forward.

Raise yourselves up into the light then you shall see the signposts of your life, your journey. For it is but a journey back to the light. For it is in God's arms that you shall lovingly reside. This is the only way forward.

To recognize the patterns each of you have formed, your life script upon the way will bring you once again into your power. Release the script that no longer serves you and raise your sights higher. You deserve to honour yourself on your journey. Would you climb a mountain laden with all your possessions? No, you would choose wisely what serves you on your journey, those tools that would enable you to move lightly and quickly forward to your destination with ease. As you strive to climb higher, so you find as the altitude becomes thinner you would choose to lighten your load. This would enable your journey to become easier.

What seemed vitally important at the bottom of the mountain would gradually cease to have any attraction. So too in your life's journey your load is weighing you down with judgements and fixed ideas. You are being crushed by your own doing choosing to hold on tight to all that does not serve you any longer.

Now make this time one of conscious choosing. Choose to lighten your load by using prayer for guidance and God will inspire you. Bring this light of the Heavens into your earthly existence and free yourself of the bonds of slavery. For indeed that is in your own doing. If you try to walk, indeed climb a mountain with chains about you, how far will you get?

Releasing and letting

go of old vibrations is the

key to moving forward

By releasing these chains of despair into the light of God you will be freed to move lightly upon your path. Fill your heart with the love of God and then step lightly and see the signposts with clarity. It is your choice how fast or slow you take upon your journey. Make this choice consciously and open up to the spiritual realms that will help you move with grace.

Releasing and letting go of old vibrations is the key to moving forward. This frees up the energy held fast in the emotional body. When this energy is static nothing can move and nothing can give. As soon as you give permission fully to free yourselves of lower vibrations, your lives will pan out before you.

It is as though on your journey you have a series of traffic lights, when you come upon a red light you can see there is no moving forward. This is then the time to cleanse afresh anything stuck in your emotional bodies. Give all that is not for the highest good up to the Heavens and ask to be released from the chains that hold you down and hold you fast. As you give permission for this to be so you will then see the red light shift to amber and the energy will propel you forward again. The way then is clear to proceed and move through the green light into a fast moving free energy.

Each of you is a master

of creating your own life

When you are in this space nothing can stop or prevent a whole series of events falling into place. From this standpoint you are back in your power and you may manifest all that is good with the highest intentions.

See your life spread before you as an empty palate. What will you fill it with? It is your choice to create beauty and harmony or to choose the rocky path of discordant energy. Each of you is a master of creating your own life. You may add or take away experiences that you so choose.

As each of you lifts your consciousness higher to bring through God's, loving guiding energy, so shall you know the way forward out of the mire and distortion of your world. It is but a thin barrier, a thin veil that you must tear through to truly see the light.

Visualize yourself in a soft cloud of bright light and as the cloud absorbs any negative energy so it is dispersed, just as a cloud dissipates and evaporates on a sunny day. See the vibration lifting higher and truly step into your power.

It shall be so for this is the kingdom of Heaven. Each of you can connect with your free will to bring this energy in to your daily lives. Be a living master of the light. Be a server of humanity to help others who are lost and cannot find their way. Let their sight be opened fully to receive the glory of God's wonder and creation.

CHAPTER SIX

You are not alone

SEE YOUR life as one drop in the ocean of Oneness. As the water moves and swirls as one body release all fear now of standing alone. It cannot be, just as in the ocean you cannot isolate one particle in the body of oneness, so you cannot separate yourself from God's flow of loving energy.

You are not alone that is just in your perception. As you tune into the elements of fear so all else is shut away. You then have closed yourself away and shut down to the greater being of God's love and kindness. Only you are responsible for putting yourself into that position. No one else can find you if you close all doors to the Oneness of God.

For as you grow and move towards the light so too it sets a shining example for others to come out of hiding. For in total truth each and every one of you has the tools, the keys to breaking down the barrier of separateness to God's love.

If you choose to stay in isolation then that is your choice. However, if you choose, indeed truly choose to move out of confinement, your own limited boundaries, then you shall move forward quickly in the flow of life in abundance. In abundance of the true value of the word, not as in monetary gain but abundance of the joy of the soul growing and expanding to the light and love of God. For abundance shall and will manifest in every way when the energy is flowing. Indeed it shall be as in a slipstream of energy. There shall be no bounds. As in the ocean of life the body of water, the expanse of water, moves as one. Where there are no dams, no rocks or stones blocking or holding back then the water shall flow unceasingly.

So too focus on this wave of loving energy, know that you are guided

Feel the presence of

God in every moment

of your lives

truly from your heart when you are connected to God's love. The expansion in you will feel as though an explosion of light filtered cells shall move through every cell and particle of your being.

Feel the presence of God in every moment of your lives. Lift up your eyes to truly see and open your hearts fully to encompass all that is in truth and God's heart. You shall then live and breathe the wonder of creation.

Now is the time to fully understand the impact of people's emotional states on the wakening up of humanity. Each and every one of you in turn has your part to play in this wheel of life. Let this not be in isolation but rather by tuning into each other's needs and being sensitive to them not critical.

You will all need to work together as a team. As you see when many work together in harmony there can be a greater outcome. Many minds shall create more impact in the energy that is put out.

See yourself as a diver alone searching the bottom of the sea for jewels of wisdom and then see a group of you together trawling the bottom of the sea. Which do you think will bring the greater fruition? Indeed it is time to work together and bring harmony into your states of mind.

Link your hands and see yourself as part of a circle coming together as one. This way you will have the force of energy to move forward. You are not alone in anyway. Tune into the greater beings of light to shine their light upon your way. This way you will follow this beacon of light upon your journey.

Bring peace and kindness to each other in everything you do. You will then see this act of service as the link to helping all of humanity move through the mire and distortion. Through times of great need and as the years unfold, you will find that you will merge and move toward each other as one.

See this as a whole and know that you are taking a larger part in what is becoming the changing of planet Earth. Hold the energy steady; beaming out your love and light to every corner of the Earth, this is the way forward. Literally saturate your mind with positive input, cast the rest away. All lower vibrations will drag you down and you will become tangled in a web unable to move freely.

Stand firm, put out your positive intention to help others and so in turn help the Earth. You will each see the movement forward however small; your hearts shall be opened.

CHAPTER SEVEN

Opening your heart

AS IN the Universe all belongs and is connected to each other, so too are all mortals upon the Earth. As amnesia has arisen amongst you, so the seeds of doubt manifest in humanity as a whole. The cries of "Where do I really come from, where am I connected, I don't feel like I belong?" As the searching goes deep within each and every one of you so it is the seeds begin to scatter and attract the answers you have longed for.

We are all One, for in the Universe all is connected. You are not separated from God. This is only through each person's imagination. It does not seem real to you anymore. The spark needs to be re-ignited; feed it love and nourish it as your parents did for you as a baby and then as a child. Each step of your life, the love and care has been there, for some more than others, but the love and spark of God have been there always. Nourish it now with your own love for it is all there is. Open your heart to God's love and the Christ within shall be freed to move you forward to truly seeing who you really are.

Let the veils of illusion dissipate and allow yourself, your true self, to be revealed. It is in so doing that you shall come into your power. It is in this way that the Light of God's loving energy shall saturate your very being.

Absorb this incredible light; breathe it into every cell and particle of your being. Then and only then shall you lead others to the Light. Not through force or persuasion but through one who knows and radiates outward God's true shining example. For others then shall be touched by the light and love that you shall truly carry deep within your soul.

Open your hearts now to receive. Receive in abundance for all of God's love shall abound and saturate you down to the smallest speck within you.

Now you may go outward in this world connected and tapped in to the Source; the Source of all God's love and wisdom. You shall then touch another's heart and as that opens love shall flow forth. The more love that is released shall hold each of you as brothers and sisters on this planet. Your planet Earth needs this love in a desperate longing to be held and nourished.

To save yourselves from extinction, which comes from drying up the core of your heart, allow your heart to crack open and be healed. See the planet inside of you and as the healing comes to your heart it shall heal the planet also. For it is not in the literal sense that extinction of you may happen, for that can never be, your soul is eternal. It is the extinction of being loveless, for then you shall wither and die in your heart. Then you will have shut down and can be of no service to yourself or others. Hold this brotherhood and sisterhood close to you, dear ones, for it is indeed a time to repent of all that has gone before on this planet. Release and let go of all that is not in Truth, Love and Light. Only then can the true forgiveness of one's own soul be complete.

For it is not judgement from God, there is no judgement there is only pure love. It is from yourselves that you hold the greatest judgement. As

Let the veils of illusion

dissipate and allow yourself,

your true self, to be revealed

you judge yourself so the jury of your mind lets you fall into a category of fear, a fear of not belonging anymore, a fear where love is not real anymore. All trust will have vanished and people feel all alone.

Reach out now to your brothers and sisters, open their hearts, open their eyes and minds to see that they are responsible for their own judge and jury. As they free themselves, so a release of freedom can be so for the Earth. Your Earth needs to be saturated in pure love and as each soul forgives themselves and cuts the ties to old habits and negative formation of ideas in their minds, so can all be renewed.

From the Light and Love of Heaven this can be done in grace. Look upward dear ones, to only see the Light, and allow all else not in the Christ's Light to fall away. As the Christ energy that is within each of you is charged, so it is like a battery of energy that will lift your vibration.

CHAPTER EIGHT

Healing

IT IS in the healing of one another that you shall see a shift in humanity. As you perceive healing to be only that of the physical, then barriers shall be put around you blocking the flow of energy. For indeed the healing that occurs in each of you is on many levels and all planes of consciousness. There may be a shift in consciousness and that is where the healing has occurred. Do not limit yourselves in your thinking but rather open up to

Your physical bodies are

but a drop in the ocean

compared to the magnitude

of the soul's journey

the greater possibilities of God's wonder. For that indeed does the ultimate in healing, allowing God's loving energy to flow through you. Give it up to the grace of God to know the areas and pockets of your very existence that need healing.

Breathe in the breath of God and in that flow of energy allow all that is good to descend upon you. It is not only the physical body that needs a shift in energy, but far greater the mind, for in the mind is stored many keys to unlock your subconscious. Once the doorways have been opened, and there shall be many of them, the cleansing shall truly begin. The energy can then sift through and disperse all negativity within it.

The cosmic healing is that which is from the truth of God. Allow it to be a possibility in your mind that all levels of consciousness need healing not only one. For in so doing you are opening up to greater expanded awareness and recognizing your existence on many levels. The shift may occur in magnitude and grace. The energy surrounding you and within you will be cleansed and purified, only then shall you see truly the healing from within. The healing shall filter through from one consciousness to the next and finally will occur in the physical body. For it is from sensations and imprints from your emotional and mental bodies that the misunderstandings have occurred.

As these are washed clean then there is no discordant energy for your physical body to feed off, the pattern and the cycle shall be broken and freed. Then and only then shall the discordant energy patterns in the physical body that have gone awry be truly healed. From this understanding all shall be revealed and the source of humanity's distress around physical illness be dispersed.

Humanity as a whole has focused too much energy on curing the physical body and other elements have been missing. Though in some fields of medicine the greater picture and greater awareness is looked at as a whole, this is minimal. The shift needs to occur in all areas of medicine to encompass the whole being. The energy frequency that each person is vibrating at, this is where the seat of disease is occurring.

With the grace of God and opening your hearts to free yourselves from all pain and despair, shall bring about a true cosmic healing. Allow the energy of Heaven to flow through you gently and dislodge the particles of energy discordant to your soul. Know that all is in perfect timing and each lesson shall occur as a gift. A gift from Heaven, for that is where your soul is nourished.

Your physical bodies are but a drop in the ocean compared to the magnitude of the soul's journey. All experiences are valid and complete in their entirety. All experiences are for your own personal growth. As there is an acceptance in this state of being then the energy from Heaven can flow through you with grace, and the healing on a multitude of levels shall occur.

Feel the essence of God's loving energy pulsating through your body saturating all of your body with Divine light. This is how each of you can connect to the Divine Source.

Each and every one of you has the spark of God's loving presence within you. It is in your own choosing whether you allow yourselves to tap into this inspiring powerful energy. For when you become a master of the light then you may radiate forth as one of God's messengers to bring healing to each other and planet Earth.

Open your hearts Beloved Ones for all to see and share in the glory of God's love. Sharing it will increase the abundance of love pouring through you. Every cell and particle of your being shall be saturated with this love. You shall see the difference in your own essence of being first and then you shall see that spark of God's love touch another. Indeed it is in so doing that the healing shall occur from one to another on the deepest level.

All that is not in truth must dissolve away for it has no place to reside in the saturation of God's love. Each of you needs to claim your power to choose to be a messenger of Divine love and light. In turn the wheel of life shall turn and the spin increase. For as the Earth's energies shall and are speeding up so the Universal energy increases, and all that is stuck in the lowest vibration of humanity shall indeed be awakened.

This is a time of choosing, stand up to be counted on the inner planes of awareness as a manifestor of God's love and light. Each step you take encourages another and so the wheel of life turns. Many mountains may be walked, those of your subconscious, to arrive at this place of power within yourself. Implode the energy of Heaven into every cell and particle of your being to stand forth to be seen from Heaven as one who carries the light as a flaming torch of Heaven's glory.

As you tap into the realms of laughter the angelic realms also delight in this energy. It is a breath of fresh air and as the saying goes 'Angels fly because they take themselves lightly'. Of course there are many factors to this but the main message is not to allow yourself to get bogged down by life and the lower energies and thought forms.

As you raise your vibration in delight the less you will want to spend any time down in the dumps. Everything seems to move much faster and you will have more energy albeit sometimes for a short space of time.

Many mountains

may be walked, those of your

subconscious, to arrive at

this place of power

within yourself

When you look at this clearly you will begin to choose more and more laughter and joy as a way of healing. As you pass this onto another it is infectious and you begin to see the joy it brings.

It is vitally important that each soul play their part to lift the sights higher for humanity. For it is in the spark of God that this energy lies to heal your planet Earth. As each soul wakes up and remembers who they truly are, then the true healing can begin within each of you and then radiate outwards to the universe.

Imagine a firework that fires upwards into the dark night sky. See it soaring upwards at great speed and then see it explode and shatter into millions upon millions of light particles lighting up the sky. See this as a symbol of each of your energy fields as you set your sights higher and seek to spread your light. As each tiny particle of light descends upon the planet it shall make a difference. Every particle and spark of the Divine that radiates outwards from the Source has the potential for great healing, whether this light descends upon the Earth itself or upon another human being it shall have an effect.

See that daily each of lifts yourself out of the doldrums and invokes the source of God's energy to radiate and touch another. This shall have a cause and effect on all it embraces. As each plant and tree in nature feels this vibrant energy it shall stir from within it the healing needed for the Earth. As it leaves an imprint of this energy so shall the healing begin in the magnificence of God's love.

Let it be your intent to use God's powerful healing energy to share with another. All shall be then sealed and healed with the love of God. You do not need to be overwhelmed by the enormousness of the planet, but rather step inside yourselves and allow the spark of God to guide you from within. This then will have an effect on the greater cosmos, far greater than you in your limited sense and understanding can achieve.

See the planet Earth radiating before you and do your part by beginning the healing from within. Then radiate outwards your light for all to share.

Letting go of old emotions

Sit quietly in the moment and begin to feel into the core of your emotions. Ask that you be shown exactly where in your physical body these are residing. Are you aware of any discomfort in any part of your body? Where you now focus your attention, there in manifest form your

Let it be your intent to

use God's powerful

healing energy to share

with another

emotions have collected into physical matter.

As you go about each day whatever energy you are focusing upon and giving your full attention so it shall be. If you fill your days lamenting about this or that from the past or any discordant non-loving energy, then so shall this start to feed through into matter. It is as though the energy around you becomes thicker and thicker and begins to suffocate certain parts of the body. For 'dis-ease' to manifest in the body so the thought forms have become magnified by the intensity with which you have carried your emotions.

It is as though a heavy cloak has descended upon you, which indeed it has. Minor attention to thoughts will produce minor effects upon your body, however it is the intensity of emotion that you carry that will weigh you down and eventually attach itself to you like glue. This vibration then becomes so dense in the physical body and may be hard to shift.

To do this takes only your intent to seek out the original emotion and ask in prayer that you be healed from this. Trust that this can be so. Really begin to feel what it is like without this heavy emotion sitting as the lead weight that it is.

As you begin to purify and cleanse your thoughts daily you will perceive a lighter energy around you. Those who come into contact with you will

Sit quietly in the moment

and begin to feel into the core

of your emotions

also sense a shift in you as the outer radiates what is deep in the inner parts of you.

Now take the time to be aware of where you are vibrating. Do you want the intense anger or fear that you are feeling to settle so deeply within your body? Checking this daily will keep you fresh in your mind and body. Release all negative emotions, you cannot afford to entertain them. Do not be surprised therefore what shows up in your life, for you are responsible in some way for their manifestation. Look deep within, as though holding a magnifying glass over yourself and begin to pinpoint the areas needing attention.

Forgiveness will be the key, for it is not to blame yourself for what has shown up in your life, but rather an acceptance. As you accept that you are creating your life by what you give attention to then so shall you be freed of lower energies.

As you begin to see the gifts in what you have learned and experienced, then so the shift can and will happen. As you would not want to hold onto a bag of rotting rubbish in your home for months on end, why then would you want to hold onto these emotions? Cleanse daily and set your sights higher, act as though you wish to be cleansed in your mind, and guidance from above will give you all the support you need. These symbols may seem harsh to you now but in time you will see with clear eyes how you have managed to change and view your life accordingly.

CHAPTER NINE

Shining your light

SEE YOURSELF not as an island all alone in the darkness, but rather as a lighthouse beaming out light in all directions into the darkness. As you shine your light for all to see however dark or dank the places you find yourself, then this light will shine to guide all others out of their darkness. It needs only one thought form to shift and gain a ripple effect throughout Man's consciousness for the healing to occur on all levels.

Stand up and feel any fear and ask that it be transmuted into the light of Christ. Then and only then may you step forward and radiate your light. For it is in the sharing and depths of your compassion for humanity that the healing shall occur on all levels of awareness. When you stand firmly and step into your power then truly each of you may become an emissary of light.

Moving forward, never static, this is the way forward for humanity. Blast through the lower consciousness of people's minds. This you do by setting the example of one who truly stands in their power. Do not be afraid to speak your truth, to open your hearts and let the love of God pour in, this is the only way forward out of the mire and distortion of your minds. When you allow your minds to take control in your lives then all chaos shall abound.

When you truly overcome these lower energies that pull you down and mislead you, then you can truly step into the light. Once you have found these keys to life you shall no longer wish to be drawn to these dark places of fear, intimidation and self-righteousness.

Let go for all shall be revealed in truth upon your journey. Each of you shall have many twists and turns upon your path, but follow your hearts and this shall lead you home to God. Do not be caught up in the drama

Do not be caught

up in the drama of life

of life. It is your choice to know that this no longer serves you to follow the crowd of humanity in self-destruction and fear. This will bring you down to the depths of despair.

Lift yourselves up and aspire to the greater parts of yourself, see your attributes and dump the rest. How can you be of service to one another when the thought forms of your mind are like a sewer of energy? Imagine trying to see your way out of this soup of your mind, how can this lead you anywhere but into more darkness?

First see the flicker of all that is good in your life or another's and let that flame grow within you. The more you focus the clearer the light shall become. As your eyes adjust to the darkness you shall see more and more. The misunderstandings in your life shall be made apparent to you, for that is all they are, misunderstandings. Now is the time to forgive yourself for these, undo the past by seeing them for what they are. For as you perceive your life, see how it is that you respond in each situation.

As a child you still have the choice but lack the maturity of adult wisdom. Go back and heal these parts of yourself by asking angelic beings of the Light to shine for you on those matters that have been buried deep in the subconscious of your mind, then you will see clearly the lessons you have chosen to learn. As you give gratitude you will see

When you stand firmly

and step into your power

then truly each of you may

become an emissary of light

them as a blessing; it is a choice in each and every situation how you respond. It is in owning this responsibility that you will move forward out of the darkness into the light and see with clarity, seeing with eyes now of wisdom and truth. In this way and from this stance you may help humanity. For as each of you heal the blocks within, the frustrations, the anger and the disappointments, so the shift can be made. As the sea of life moves in accordance with the Universal Laws, so all shall be revealed and healed.

Your thoughts...

To find out more about Annie's work and other publications
visit www.higher-realms.co.nz